D1249483

# Chimpanzees

## Patricia Kendell

 RAINTREE
STECK-VAUGHN
PUBLISHERS

A Harcourt Company

Austin   New York
www.raintreesteckvaughn.com

# Chimpanzees Dolphins Elephants
# Lions Polar Bears Tigers

Published by Raintree Steck-Vaughn Publishers, an imprint of Steck-Vaughn Company

**Library of Congress Cataloging-in-Publication Data**

Kendell, Patricia.
  Chimpanzees / Patricia Kendell.
    p. cm.—(In the wild)
  Includes bibliographical references (p.).
  Summary: Photographs and simple text introduce the behavior and habitat of chimpanzees, and a list of resources provides organizations, books, and websites which deal with helping to protect them.
    ISBN 0-7398-4904-2
    1. Chimpanzees—Juvenile literature. [1. Chimpanzees.]
    I. Title.II. Series.

QL737.P96 K34 2002
599.885—dc21                                    2001048966

Printed in Hong Kong. Bound in the United States.

1 2 3 4 5 6 7 8 9 0 LB 06 05 04 03 02

Photograph acknowledgments:
Bruce Coleman 3 (second & third), 4, 9, 15, 17, 24; FLPA 12 (Minden Pictures), 13 (T Whittaker), 19 (Michael Gore), 3 (fourth), 25 (Jurgen & Christine Sohns), 26 (Brake/Sunset); NHPA 28 (Martin Harvey), 11, 16, 20 (Steve Robinson), 18 (Nigel J Dennis);Oxford Scientific Films 5 (Mike Birkhead), 10 (Konrad Wothe), 29 (Clive Bromhall);Science Photo Library 3 (first), 14, 21 (Tom McHugh), 22 (Tim Davis);Still Pictures 1, 8, 23, 32 (Michel Gunther), 7 (John Cancalosi), 27 (Paul Harrison); WWF  D Lawson 6.

# Contents

# Where Chimpanzees Live

Chimpanzees live in tropical regions of Western and Central Africa.

Of all the animals in the world, they are the ones most like people. They show joy, anger, and sadness in their faces and even hug and kiss!

# Baby Chimpanzees

This proud mother is holding her tiny new baby. Like newborn humans, baby chimpanzees can do nothing for themselves at first.

For at least five years, they will stay close to their mother. She provides her babies with food, warmth, and protection.

# Looking After the Babies

Chimpanzees take care of their babies and love them very much. This baby is giving its mother a kiss.

8

Baby chimpanzees quickly learn how to cling onto their mother's fur. They ride from place to place on their mother's back until they are older.

# Family Life

Chimpanzees live together in **troops**.
The strongest male chimpanzee will become the leader.

This chimpanzee shows that he is the leader of the troop by acting fiercely to scare away other males.

# Grooming

Adult chimpanzees **groom** their babies to keep their fur clean and free from insects. This is just one of the ways the adults care for their young.

Adult chimpanzees groom one another, too.

# Growing Up

Mother chimpanzees teach their babies where to find food and how to make a nest.

These young chimpanzees have found food
that is good to eat.

# Making Friends

Young chimpanzees love to play together.
This helps them to grow strong.

Like people, chimpanzees' faces tell you when they are angry, sad, excited, or frightened. These chimps look as if they are thinking about something.

# Eating

Chimpanzees eat mainly fruit and leaves. But they also like insects and will sometimes kill small animals like pigs.

Chimpanzees hunt early in the morning and in the afternoon. This group is moving through the forest looking for food.

# Using Tools

Chimpanzees learn how to use tools from the adults. This chimp is digging **termites** out of the ground with a stick.

Chimpanzees get most
of the water they need
from juicy fruit. This
thirsty chimp is using
a leaf to scoop up water.

# Rest and Sleep

This group is resting in the middle of the day.

This chimpanzee has made a nest of branches and leaves, high up in a tree. It will sleep here at night, out of reach of danger.

# Chimpanzees in Danger

This chimpanzee is giving an alarm call because there is a leopard nearby.

This mother is protecting her baby from enemies.

# People and Chimpanzees

People are cutting down more and more trees for wood and to make room for crops. Because of this, chimpanzees are losing their forest homes.

Young chimpanzees are captured and **smuggled** to other
countries. They are sold as pets, or used for **medical research**.

# Helping Chimpanzees to Survive

These **orphan** babies have been rescued because they will not be able to survive alone in the wild. Keepers teach them some of the skills they would have learned from their mothers.

28

These chimpanzees are safe because they live in a part of the rain forest that has been made into a **wildlife reserve**. Here, all the trees and animals are properly fed and protected.

# Further Information

Find out more about how we can help chimpanzees in the future.

## ORGANIZATIONS TO CONTACT

**The Jane Goodall Institute**
Attention: SBL
P.O. Box 14890
Silver Spring, MD 20911

**International Primate Protection League**
P.O. Box 766
Summerville, SC 29484

**World Wildlife Fund**
1250 Twenty-South NW
P.O. Box 97180
Washington, D.C. 20077-7180

## BOOKS

Banks, Martin. *Chimpanzees: Habitats, Life Cycles, Food Chains, Threats*. New York: Raintree Steck-Vaughn, 2000.

Farbman, Melinda and Frye Gaillard. *Spacechimp: NASA's Ape in Space*. Berkeley Heights, NJ: Enslow Publishers, Incorporated, 2000.

Goodall, Jane. *With Love*. New York: North-South Books, 1998.

Goodall, Jane. *My Life with the Chimpanzees*. Seattle, WA: Minstrel Books, 2000.

Grunberg, Daniel A. *Chimpanzees*. Estes Park, CO: Benchmark Books, 2000.

Head, Honor. *What's It Like to Be a Chimp?* Brookfield, CT: Millbrook Press, Incorporated, 1998.

McDonald, Mary Ann. *Chimpanzees*. Chanhassen, MN: Childs World, 1998.

Robinson, Claire. *Chimpanzees*. Crystal Lake, IL: Heinemann Library, 2001.

# Glossary

## WEBSITES

www.savethechimps.org

The Center for Captive Chimp Care was established by Jane Goodall and Roger Fouts in 1997 to provide a sanctuary for chimpanzees. The website provides facts about chimps and how to adopt orphans.

www.panda.org/kids/wildlife

WWF's virtual wildlife pages provide facts about chimpanzees, how their survival is threatened and what can be done about it.

**groom** – to clean. Chimpanzees pick out dust and insects from each other's fur.

**orphan** – (OR-fuhn) a young animal whose parents have died.

**medical research** – (MED-uh-kuhl REE-surch) work done by scientists to find cures for diseases.

**smuggled** – (SMUHG-uhld) taken away in secret, often against the law.

**termites** – (TUR-mites) white ants that eat wood.

**troop** – a group of chimpanzees living together.

**wildlife reserve** – (WILDE-life ri-SURV) a safe place where wild animals can live.

# Index

32

Saunders